Anonymous

Laws of Maine Relating to Public Schools

1899

Anonymous

Laws of Maine Relating to Public Schools
1899

ISBN/EAN: 9783337232368

Printed in Europe, USA, Canada, Australia, Japan

Cover: Foto ©Suzi / pixelio.de

More available books at **www.hansebooks.com**

LAWS OF MAINE

RELATING TO

PUBLIC SCHOOLS.

1899.

Compiled by the State Superintendent, and printed agreeably to An Act
approved March 9, 1889.

AUGUSTA
KENNEBEC JOURNAL PRINT
1899

PUBLIC SCHOOLS,

Being Chapter 11, Revised Statutes of 1883, as amended by subsequent legislation, governing the management of all public schools except those in districts organized with special powers by acts of Legislature.

---

*Sect. 1. The school districts in all towns in this state are hereby abolished. Provided, however, that school districts organized with special powers by act of the legislature, may retain such organization and special powers; but said districts shall annually, on or before the first day of June, by their agents, trustees or directors, submit to the school committees of their several towns estimates of the amount required for the maintenance of the schools therein, other than free high schools, for the ensuing school year, and shall be entitled to such portion of the common school-funds of the town as said committees shall determine, which sum shall not be less than is necessary for the maintenance of their schools for a period equal to that of the other schools of the town. *(School districts abolished. —exception, in case of specially chartered districts. —provisions in such cases.)*

The corporate powers of every school district shall continue under this act so far as the same may be necessary for the meeting of its liabilities and the enforcing of its rights; and any property held in trust by any school district by virtue of a gift, devise or *(—corporate powers necessary for enforcement of rights and meeting obligations, continued.)*

---

* Comprising sections 1 and 4 of chapter 216, Public Laws of 1893.

bequest for the benefit of said district shall continue
to be held and used according to the terms thereof.

*Sect. 2. Immediately after this act shall have
become a law, towns shall take possession of all
schoolhouses, lands, apparatus and other property
owned and used by the school districts hereby
abolished, which districts may lawfully sell and convey. The property so taken shall forthwith be appraised by the assessors of said towns, and at the first
annual assessment thereafter a tax shall be levied
upon the whole town, or such part thereof as is in-
cluded within the districts abolished, equal to the
whole of said appraisal, and there shall be remitted
to the tax payers of each of said districts the said
appraised value of its property so taken. In case of
districts comprising parts of two or more towns, the
assessors of said towns shall jointly appraise the
school property belonging to said districts, and shall
determine the part thereof belonging to each of the
said towns, and each town shall remit to the tax
payers in its part of such district the part so determined, in the same manner as in case of districts
wholly within said town; except that cities or towns,
which have or shall reimburse districts or parts of
districts for their school property, shall receive for the
use of such city or town, the money to which such
districts or parts of districts shall be entitled under
this act.

†Sect. 3. This act shall not abolish or change
the location of any school legally established at the
time of its passage; but any town at its annual meeting, or at a meeting called for the purpose, may determine the number and location of its schools, and
may discontinue them or change their location; but
such discontinuance or change of location shall be
made only on the written recommendation of the
superintending school committee, and on conditions
proper to preserve the just rights and privileges of

Marginal notes:
Town, to take posses- sion of school property.

—appraisal thereof, to be made.

—tax there- for, to be assessed.

—remittance, to be made to tax-payers of each district.

—procedure, in case of dis- tricts com- prising parts of two or more towns.

No school abolished, or location thereof changed, except by vote of town on recom- mendation of school committee.

---

*Section 2 of chapter 216, Public Laws of 1893.
†Section 3 of chapter 216, Public Laws of 1893 as amended by chapter 285, Public Laws of 1897, and by chapters 48 and 74, Public Laws
of 1899.

the inhabitants for whose benefit such schools were established, provided, however, that in any case of any school having, as now established, or which shall hereafter have, too few scholars for its profitable maintenance, the superintending school committee may suspend the operation of such school for not more than one year, unless otherwise instructed by the town, but any public school failing to maintain an average attendance for any school year, of at least eight pupils, shall be and hereby is suspended, unless the town in which said school is located shall by vote instruct its superintending school committee to maintain said school. The superintendent of schools in each town shall procure the conveyance of all public school pupils residing in his town, to and from the nearest suitable school, for the number of weeks for which schools are maintained in each year, when such pupils reside at such a distance from the said schools as in the judgment of the superintending school committee shall render such conveyance necessary. Provided, however, that the superintending school committee may authorize the superintendent of schools to pay the board of any pupil or pupils at a suitable place near any established school, instead of providing conveyance for said pupil or pupils, when in their judgment it may be done at an equal or less expense than by conveyance.

—school committee, may suspend small schools.

—any school having an average of less than eight is discontinued unless continued by vote of the town.

—superintendent of schools must procure conveyance of all scholars who reside so far from schools as to render it necessary, or may board scholars near schools.

*Sect. 4. The school-moneys of every town shall be so expended as to give as nearly as practicable the same aggregate annual length of terms in all its schools, and every town shall make provision for the maintenance of all its schools for not less than twenty weeks annually. Any town failing to maintain its schools as provided in this section, shall be debarred from drawing its state school-moneys, till it shall have made suitable provisions for so maintaining them thereafter.

Schools shall all be of same length, and not less than 20 weeks per year.

—penalty, for failure to thus maintain schools.

*Sect. 5. Adjoining towns, upon the written recommendation of the school committee of said towns, may by concurrent action maintain union

Union schools, may be maintained.

* Sections 5 and 6 of chapter 216, Public Laws of 1893.

schools for the benefit of parts of said towns in what are now union school districts, or may establish such schools, and shall contribute to their support each in

—manner of support. proportion to the number of scholars in each of said towns attending such schools. Said schools shall be

—management. under the management of the school committee of the town in which their schoolhouses are located.

Towns, to raise for schools 80 cents per inhabitant. Sect. 6. Every town shall raise and expend, annually, for the support of schools therein, exclusive of the income of any corporate school-fund, or of any grant from the revenue of funds from the state, or of any voluntary donation, devise or bequest, or of any forfeiture accruing to the use of schools, not less than eighty cents for each inhabitant, according to the

—penalty census by which representatives to the legislature were last apportioned, under penalty of forfeiting not less than twice nor more than four times the amount of its deficiency.

School-fund and mill tax to be withheld from delinquent towns. *'Sect. 7. When the governor and council have reason to believe that a town has neglected to raise and expend the school money required by law, or to examine teachers as prescribed by law, or to have instruction given in the subjects prescribed by law or to provide suitable text books in the subjects prescribed by law, or faithfully to expend the school money received from the state, they shall direct the treasurer of state to withhold further payment to such town from the state school fund and mill tax until such town satisfies them that it has expended the full amount of school money required by law.

Towns, shall provide school-books, for both common and Free High Schools. † Sect. 8. Towns shall provide school-books, apparatus and appliances for the use of the pupils in the public schools, including all free high schools, at the expense of said town; and shall also pay for the necessary repairs of school-buildings and insurance on same, if any, improvement and maintenance of school yards and playgrounds out of a sum or sums of money raised and appropriated for that pur-

---

* As amended by chapter 64, Public Laws of 1899.
† As amended by chapter 268, Public Laws of 1889, and further amended by chapter 260, Public Laws of 1897.

pose which shall be assessed like other moneys; pro- *Repairs, insurance, &c., cannot be paid for from school-fund.* vided, however, that any parent or guardian of any pupil in the public schools may, at his own expense, procure for the separate and exclusive use of such pupil, the text-books required to be used in such schools.

* Sect. 9. School committees shall make such *Distribution and preservation of books.* rules and regulations not repugnant to law, as they deem proper, for the distribution and preservation of school-books and appliances furnished at the expense of the town.

Sect. 10. When a pupil in the public school loses, *School-books, damages for injuring or destroying, how recovered of parent, etc.* destroys, or unnecessarily injures any such school-book or appliance, furnished such pupil at the expense of said town, his parent or guardian shall be notified, and if the loss or damage is not made good to the satisfaction of such committee within a reasonable time, they shall report the case to the assessors, who shall include in the next town tax of the delinquent parent or guardian the value of the book or appliance so lost, destroyed or injured, to be assessed and collected as other town taxes.

† Sect. 11. Any city or town may annually make *Cities and towns, may instruct in industrial or mechanical drawing, and may support evening schools.* provision for free instruction in industrial or mechanical drawing, to persons over fifteen years of age, either in day or evening schools, under direction of the superintending school committee. Cities and towns may raise and appropriate money for the support of evening schools in addition to the sum they raise for the support of common schools. Said evening schools shall admit persons of any age, shall teach only the elementary branches and shall be under the direction and supervision of the local school board.

Sect. 12. (Repealed by chapter 216, Public Laws of 1893.)

‡ Sect. 13. The assessors or municipal officers of *Certificate of cities, towns, &c., to be returned annually to* each town, shall, on or before the first day of each May, make to the state superintendent of public

---

* As amended by chapter 268, Public Laws of 1889.

† As amended by chapter 246, Public Laws of 1889.

‡ As amended by chapter 237, Public Laws of 1897.

State super-intendent. schools, a certificate, under oath, embracing the following items:

Amount voted by town. I. The amount voted by the town for common schools at preceding annual meeting.

—payable from state. II. The amount of school-moneys payable to the town from the state treasury during the year ending with the first day of the preceding April.

—expended for schools. III. The amount of money actually expended for common schools during the last school year.

—unex-pended. IV. The amount of school-moneys unexpended, whether in the town treasury or in the hands of district agents.

V. Answers to such other inquiries as are presented to secure a full and complete statement of school revenues and expenditures.

Blanks furnished to towns. Sect. 14. The state superintendent shall prepare and furnish to the town officers such blanks as he deems proper to secure the fiscal returns required in

—superintendent to make return to state treasurer. the preceding section. He shall return to the treasurer of state on the first day of July, annually, a list of such towns as have made such fiscal returns;

—money withheld from delinquent towns. and no school-moneys shall be paid by the treasurer of state to any town, so long as it neglects to make such returns.

Sections 15 and 16 (Repealed by chapter 216, Public Laws of 1893.)

School money, how paid by towns. Sect. 17. No money appropriated by law for public schools shall be paid from the treasury of any town, except upon the written order of its municipal

—how avouched. officers; and no such order shall be drawn by said officers, except upon presentation of a properly vouched bill of items.

Town, to choose superintending school committee. * Sect. 18. Every town shall choose by ballot at its annual meeting, a superintending school committee of three, to hold office as provided in section eighty-six and shall fill vacancies arising therein at

—sex, no test of eligibility. each subsequent annual meeting. No person is ineligible to the office of superintending school committee on account of sex.

* As amended by chapter 216, Public Laws of 1893, and further amended by chapter 327, Public Laws of 1897.

Sect. 19.   (Repealed by chapter 216, Public Laws of 1893.)

†Sect. 20.   A town failing to elect members of superintending school committee as required by law, forfeits not less than thirty nor more than two hundred dollars. Neglect to choose committee or superintendent.

‡Sect. 21.   The age of pupils allowed to attend the public schools of this state is hereby fixed between the ages of five and twenty-one years of age.   Any person between the age of five and twenty-one years living at any light station not embraced within the limits of any school district, shall be admitted to any public school in this state without paying tuition. Such scholars shall be entitled to all privileges and benefits, and be subject to the same conditions, rules and regulations as scholars residing in the district in which they attend school.   Towns may make such by-laws, not repugnant to law, concerning habitual truants, and children between six and seventeen years of age not attending school, without any regular and lawful occupation, and growing up in ignorance, as are most conducive to their welfare and the good order of society; and may annex a suitable penalty, not exceeding twenty dollars, for any breach thereof; but such by-laws must be first approved by a judge of the supreme judicial court. Right to attend school, defined.
Towns, to make by-laws concerning truants,
—penalty.

Sect. 22.   Such towns shall, at their annual meeting, appoint one or more persons, who alone shall make complaints for violations of said by-laws, and shall execute the judgments of the magistrate. Who shall complain of violation of by-laws.

Sect. 23.   Said magistrate, in place of fine, may order children proved to be growing up in truancy, and without the benefit of the education provided for them by law, to be placed for such periods as he thinks expedient, in the institution of instruction, house of reformation, or other suitable situation provided for the purpose under section twenty-one. Truant children, in suitable institutions.

† As amended by chapter 216, Public Laws of 1893.
‡ As amended by chapters 162 and 199, Public Laws of 1893.

*COMPULSORY EDUCATION.

Children between ages of 7 and 15 years, shall attend public school at least 16 weeks annually

Sect. 24. Every child between the ages of seven and fifteen inclusive shall attend some public day school during the time such school is in session; provided that necessary absence may be excused by the superintending school committee or superintendent of schools or teacher acting by direction of either; provided, also, that such attendance shall not be required if the child obtain equivalent instruction, for a like period of time, in an approved private school or in any other manner approved by the superintending school committee; and provided further, that the superintending school committee may exclude from the public schools any child whose physical or mental condition makes it inexpedient for him to attend. All persons having children under their control shall cause them to attend school as provided in this section, and for every neglect of such duty **—penalty for neglect.** shall forfeit a sum not exceeding twenty-five dollars, to the treasurer of the city or town, for the use of the public schools of such city or town, or shall be imprisoned not exceeding thirty days.

—children, may attend school in adjoining town.

Children living remote from any public school in the town in which they reside may be allowed to attend the public schools in an adjoining town, under such regulations and on such terms as the school committees of said towns agree upon and prescribe, and the school committee of the town in which such children reside shall pay the sum agreed upon, out of the appropriations of money raised in said town for school purposs. Except as above provided, a child attending a public school in a town in which his parent or legal guardian does not reside, after having obtained the consent of the school committee of such town, shall pay, as tuition, a sum equal to the average expense per scholar in such school.

Cities and towns, shall elect truant officers.

† Sect. 25. Cities and towns shall annually elect one or more persons, to be designated truant officers,

---

* Chapter 80, Public Laws of 1899.
† As amended by chapter 80, Public Laws of 1899.

who shall inquire into all causes of neglect of the duties prescribed in section one and ascertain the reasons therefor, and shall promptly report the same to the superintending school committee, and such truant officers, or any of them shall, when so directed by the school committee or superintendent in writing, prosecute in the name of the city or town, any person liable to the penalty provided in said section; and said officers shall have power, and it shall be their duty, when notified by any teacher that any pupil is irregular in attendance to arrest and take such pupil to school when found truant; and further it shall be the duty of such officers to enforce the provisions of sections one hundred and fourteen to one hundred and sixteen, inclusive, of chapter eleven of the revised statutes. Every city or town neglecting to elect truant officers, and truant officers neglecting to prose- —duties. cutte when directed, as required by law, shall for- feit not less than ten nor more than fifty dollars, to the use of the public schools in the city or town neg- lecting as aforesaid, or to the use of the public schools in the city or town where such truant officer resides.

The municipal officers shall fix the compensation —compensation of truant of the truant officers, elected as prescribed in this officers. section. Superintending school committees shall —committee may fill have power to fill vacancies occurring during the vacancies. year.

Sect. 26. If a child, without sufficient excuse, Habitual truant shall be absent from school six or more times during defined. any term, he shall be deemed an habitual truant, and the superintending school committee shall notify him and any person under whose control he may be that —how unless he conforms to section one of this act, the pro- punished. visions of the two following sections will be enforced against them; and if thereafter such child continues irregular in attendance, the truant officers or any of them shall, when so directed by the school committee or superintendent in writing, enforce said provisions by complaint.

Any person having control of a child who is Persons an habitual truant, as defined in the foregoing encouraging

truancy how punished. section, and being in any way responsible for such truancy, and any person who induces a child to absent himself from school, or harbors or conceals such child when he is absent shall forfeit not exceeding twenty dollars, for the use of the public schools of the city or town in which such child resides, to be recovered by the truant officer on complaint, or shall be imprisoned not exceeding thirty days.

Habitual truant may be sent to Reform School or Industrial School for Girls. On complaint of the truant officer, an habitual truant, if a boy, may be committed to the state reform school, or, if a girl, to the state industrial school for girls, or to any truant school that may hereafter be established.

Jurisdiction of officers. Sect. 27. Police or municipal courts and trial justices shall have jurisdiction of the offences described in sections twenty-four, twenty-five and twenty-six.

FREE HIGH SCHOOLS.

State aid to free high school. *Sect. 28. Any town which establishes and maintains a free high school as provided by this section and the seven following, for at least ten weeks in any one year, shall, on complying with the conditions hereinafter set forth, receive from the state one-half

—amount. the amount actually expended for instruction in said

—proviso. school, not exceeding two hundred and fifty dollars; *provided*, that no town shall receive such state aid unless its appropriation and expenditure for such school, has been exclusive of the amounts required by law for common school purposes. Such aid shall be paid from the state treasury on and after the first

—how paid. day of each December, upon certification by the governor and council as provided by section thirty-five. But whenever a town or precinct desires to draw its state aid semi-annually, it shall be paid on and after the first days of June and December; *pro-*

—proviso. *vided*, that the superintendent of such town makes, semi-annually, before said days, the report required in section thirty-five.

---

*As amended by chapter 216, Public Laws of 1893.

*Sect. 29. Any town may establish and maintain not exceeding two free high schools; and in such case shall receive the same state aid as if the expenditures of both schools had been made for one. Two or more adjoining towns may unite in establishing and maintaining a free high school, and both shall receive the same state aid as if such school had been maintained by one town. So long as any town declines to avail itself of the foregoing provisions, the inhabitants of any section of said town may organize a free high school precinct in the manner hereinafter provided, which may establish and maintain a free high school, and receive state aid the same as the town might have done; *provided*, that no more than two such free high schools shall be established in any town, and that the amount of aid extended to the precincts in any town shall not exceed the sum that the town might have received. On petition of any five voters resident in said section, reciting the limits of the precinct proposed, the municipal officers of the town shall call a meeting of the voters within said limits by causing notices, specifying the time, place and purposes of said meeting, seven days before the time appointed, to be posted in two or more conspicuous places within said limits. Said meeting shall choose a moderator and a clerk who shall be sworn, and shall, by a majority vote of those present and voting, determine whether said precinct shall be organized. It shall choose an agent who shall be duly sworn, whose powers and duties shall be as hereinafter defined. Such precinct may continue its organization from year to year by the holding of meetings called in the manner aforesaid, so long as the town shall neglect or refuse to support free high schools. Sections of adjoining towns may organize as herein provided and may establish and maintain a union free high school, and, with the consent of both towns, may receive a proportional part of such aid, to be determined as provided by section

Marginal notes:
Free high schools, any town may establish two.

—adjoining towns, may maintain school.

—precincts, may be organized and established.

—proviso.

—sections of adjoining towns, may organize precincts, and maintain, receive and expend donations and bequests.

* As amended by chapter 216, Public Laws of 1893.

thirty-five, but in no case to exceed the amount that either town might have received. But no more than two such precincts shall exist at the same time in any town. Moneys voted by said precincts shall be assessed and collected in the manner now provided for assessment and collection of moneys voted by school districts. Towns shall receive in trust and faithfully expend gifts and bequests made to aid in the maintenance of free high schools, and shall receive aid in such cases to the same extent and on the same conditions as if such schools had been established and maintained by taxation; and any town or district shall receive such state aid on any expenditure for a free high school or schools, made from the funds or proceeds of the real estate of an academy or incorporated institution of learning, surrendered or transferred to such town or district for educational purposes; but if any part of the money so paid by the state is expended for any other purpose than the support of such free high schools, as provided by this section, then each person so misapplying said money forfeits double the sum so misapplied, to be recov-

—penalty, for misapplying money appropriated by state.

ered in an action of debt, in the name and to the use of the town, by any inhabitant thereof; and no town shall receive further support from the state for any free high school, until the amount so received, but misapplied, has been raised and expended for such free high schools by such town.

Location.

*Sect. 30. Any town, or union of towns, precinct or union of precincts, voting to establish a free high school as herein provided, may locate the same permanently, or vote that the terms thereof be held alter-

—school-rooms, &c., how supplied and furnished.

nately in such sections or precincts within the town or towns as may be selected, and as may accept said school. The precinct in which said school is thus held, shall supply appropriate equipments, and furnish a warm and suitable building for the same; pro-

—proviso.

vided, that such precinct may use its school house or school houses for such free high school, when not required for ordinary school purposes.

* As amended by chapter 216, Public Laws of 1893.

* Sect. 31. The course of study in the free high schools shall embrace the ordinary English academic studies which are taught in secondary schools, especially the natural sciences in their application to mechanics, manufactures and agriculture; but the ancient or modern languages and music shall not be taught therein except by direction of the superintending school committees having supervision thereof. Such schools, when established by any town or union of towns, shall be free to all the youth in such town or towns who have such scholastic attainments as will fit them to attend such schools with profit, and the superintendent, or superintending school committee, having supervision thereof shall make such examination of candidates for admission to said schools as they consider necessary. When such school is established by any precinct or union of precincts, it shall be free in the same manner to the scholars within such precincts, and open also to scholars passing the required examination from without such precincts, but within the towns in which said precincts are situated, on payment to the agent of the precinct in which such school is located, of such tuition, to be fixed by the superintending school committee or committees having supervision of the same, as is equivalent to the cost a scholar of maintaining such school, after deducting the aid extended by the state. Whenever in the judgment of the superintending school committees having the supervision of any free high school or schools, the number of pupils in the same may be increased without detriment, scholars from without the towns directly interested in such school or schools, may be admitted to the same on passing the required examination and paying such tuition as may be fixed by such committee, to the treasurer of the town in which the school is kept, when the school is maintained by a town or union of towns, or to the agent of the precinct in which the

course of study, what it shall embrace.

—exception.

—schools, to be free to youth in town or district.

—S. S. committees, may admit pupils from without town on payment of tuition.

---

* As amended by chapters 100 of the Public Laws of 1887, 212 of the Public Laws of 1889, 216 of the Public Laws of 1893, and 299 of the Public Laws of 1897.

school is kept, when such school is maintained by a precinct or union of precincts.

Free high schools, subject to the school laws, except in certain cases.

*Sect. 32. Free high schools, established and maintained under the foregoing provisions, are subject to the laws relating to common schools, so far as applicable, except as otherwise provided. When

—established by towns, how managed.

established and maintained by a town, they shall be under the supervision and entire management of the superintending school committee of such town.

—established by union of towns.

When established and maintained by a union of towns, such school shall be under the supervision and entire management of the school committees of such towns, who constitute a joint board for that purpose.

—established by districts.

When established and maintained by any precinct or union of precincts in the same town, such schools shall be under the supervision of the superintending committee of such town, or of the state superintendent, when the precinct or precincts so elect, and under the financial management of the agent of the precinct in which such school is kept, who, in connection with said committee or superintendent, shall

—established by districts in different towns.

employ teachers for the same. When established and maintained by two precincts in different towns, such school shall be under the supervision of the superintending school committees of such towns, who constitute a joint board for that purpose, and under the financial management of the agents of both precincts, who, in connection with said committees, shall employ the teachers.

Towns, may raise money to maintain free high schools.

*Sect. 33. Towns and precincts may raise money for establishing and maintaining free high schools and erecting buildings and providing equipments for the same, in the same manner as for supporting common schools and erecting schoolhouses.

Towns, may contract with and pay academies and high schools for tuition of scholars.

† Sect. 34. Any town may from year to year authorize its superintending school committee to contract with and pay the trustees of any academy in said town for the tuition of scholars within such town, in

---

* As amended by chapter 216, Public Laws of 1893.

† As amended by chapter 167, Public Laws of 1889, and by chapter 6, Public Laws of 1899.

the studies contemplated by the six preceding sec- —joint committee provided for.
tions, under a standard of scholarship to be estab-
lished by such committee; and when such contract
has been made, the school committee with an equal
number from the board of trustees of such academy —entitled to state aid for expenditure.
shall form a joint committee for the selection of all
teachers, and the arranging of the course of study in
such academy, when such academy has less than ten
teousand dollars endowment; and the expenditure of
any town for tuition in such academy shall be subject
to the same conditions, and shall entitle such towns
to the same state aid as if it had made such expenditure for a free high school.

*Sect. 35. Superintendents shall, annually, before Superintendents to make annual return to state superintendent.
the first day of June, make returns under oath to the
state superintendent, on blanks prepared and sent out
by him, of the amount appropriated and the amount
expended by each town or precinct for instruction in
such free high schools during the current year; also
of the amount appropriated and the amount expended for common school purposes by each town
maintaining the same; the number of weeks during
which such schools have been taught; the wages paid
each teacher; the number of pupils registered; the
average attendance; the number of pupils in each
branch of study pursued, and the amount received —state superintendent, to certify amounts to which towns are entitled.
for tuition. If the state superintendent is satisfied
that the provisions of the seven preceding sections
have been complied with, he shall certify to the governor and council the sum which each town or precinct
is entitled to receive from the state. Any town or
precinct, dissatisfied with his decision, may appeal
to the governor and council. The goveror and coun- —governor and council, to certify amounts to treasurer.;
cil shall issue a certificate to the treasurer of the
town, or agent of the precinct, for such amount as
they adjudge such town or precinct entitled to receive from the state treasury. Any person con-
nected with the management of such free high —penalty, for defrauding state.
schools, either as teacher, agent or superintendent,

*As amended by chapter 216, Public Law of 1889. 2

who in any way aids or abets in defrauding the state
into the **payment in** support of said schools of more
than is contemplated by this chapter, shall forfeit not
less than five hundred dollars, or be imprisoned in the
county jail not less than one year.

Trustees of academies, &c., may surrender property to establish free high schools. Sect. 36. **The trustees** of any academy **or other**
corporation formed for educational purposes may by
a majority vote of such of said trustees as reside in
the state, surrender the whole, **or** any part of the
property belonging thereto, to the municipal officers
of any town, or the trustees of any school-fund in any
town in which said academy or corporation is situated, for turning **the** same into a **free** high school as
hereinafter provided, and said municipal officers or
—trustees of free high schools, duties of. trustees, for the time being, shall be a board of trustees to take **and** hold said property for maintaining
a free high school; and upon receiving said **property,**
they shall use proper diligence to **make the same**
produce income for the support **of** said **free high**
school.

Property, how conveyed. Sect. 37. When such vote is so passed, **the treas-**
urer of said trustees shall convey, assign and deliver
to the municipal officers of said town, or the trustees
of such fund, **all** property belonging to said academy
or corporation for the purposes indicated by the preceding **section.**

Income of property, how applied. Sect. 38. The municipality accepting the prop-
erty in trust, as named in section thirty-six, **shall**
apply the income thereof towards the support of a
free high school, to be kept within said municipality,
at least twenty-two weeks in each year, and provide
suitable accommodations for the same and the superintending school committee or superintendent in
said municipality shall determine the qualifications
—qualification of pupils, how determined. necessary to entitle any applicant to enter or attend
said free high school, and no one shall attend it with-
out the certificate of said officers to that effect.

Tuition, to be paid by non-residents. Sect. 39. All scholars residing within the municipality aforesaid, having **such** certificate, may attend
said school without tuition fee, and all scholars not

residents of said municipality, may attend said school, upon such terms and conditions as said school officers impose.

POWERS AND OBLIGATIONS OF SCHOOL DISTRICTS.

Sections 40 to 55 inclusive. (Repealed by chapter 216, Public Laws of 1893, except so far as applicable to districts not abolished by section 1 of said chapter, and to precincts formed for maintenance of **free high** schools under provisions of section **7 of said** chapter.)

SCHOOLHOUSES, LOCATION AND ERECTION OF.

*Sect. 56. The location for the erection or removal of schoolhouses **and** requisite buildings and for playgrounds shall **be** designated by **vote** of the town at any town meeting called for that purpose. — Location for school houses, shall be designated by vote of town.

Sect. 57. When a **location for** the erection or removal of a schoolhouse and requisite buildings **has** been legally designated, **and the** owner thereof refuses to sell, or, in the opinion **of** the municipal officers, asks an unreasonable **price** for it, or resides without the state and has no authorized **attorney or agent therein,** they may lay out a schoolhouse lot, not exceeding **one** hundred square rods, and **appraise** the damages, **as** is provided for laying **out town** ways and appraising **the** damages therefor; and on payment or tender **of such** damages, **or if such** owner does not reside in the state, upon depositing such damages in the **treasury** of such **town or district** for his use, **the** town or district designating it may take such lot to be held **and** used for the **purposes** aforesaid; and when **such** schoolhouse **has** ceased to be thereon **for two years,** said **lot** reverts to the owner, his heirs **or assigns.** And any town or city may take real estate for the enlargement or extension of any location designated for the erection or removal of a — Towns may lay out school house lots in certain cases.

—damages, how appraised.

—how paid.

—lots to revert to owner, if not occupied for two years.

—land, may be taken for school house

* As amended by chapter 216, Public Laws of 1893.

lots, play-grounds, etc., not within fifty feet of a dwelling. schoolhouse and requisite buildings and play grounds, as herein provided; but no real estate shall be so taken within fifty feet of a dwelling house.

Owners aggrieved, issue may be tried by jury. *Sect. 58. If the owner is aggrieved at the location of the lot, or the damages awarded, he may apply to the county commissioners within one year, who may change the location and assess the damages, and the proceedings shall be conducted as in section eight, of chapter eighteen. If the damages are increased, or the location changed, such town shall pay the damages and costs; otherwise the costs shall be paid by the applicant.

Schoolhouse lots, erroneous location of re-established and made valid. *Sect. 59. Any town which, by its officers or by a committee, has designated, located and described a lot upon which to erect, move or repair a schoolhouse, and from mistake or omission has failed to comply with the law, whereby such location has been rendered invalid, may, on petition of three legal voters and taxpayers thereof, apply in writing to the selectmen of said town, and have the lot, so designated or described, reappraised by them.

Notice of appraisement and hearing, to be given. *Sect. 60. The selectmen of any town to whom such application has been made, shall forthwith give not less than seven nor more than twenty days' notice, to the owner of such real estate, or to the persons having the same in charge, of the time and place by them fixed for such hearing, and shall, after examination and hearing of all interested, appraise the lot as set out and affix a fair value thereon, exclusive of improvements made by said town either by buildings or otherwise; and shall, as soon as practicable, notify the persons interested in said estate who had been notified as hereinbefore provided, of the sum at which said lot has been appraised.

Sum, how assessed and collected. Sect. 61. The sum fixed as the value of said lot shall be assessed, collected and paid over as provided in section fifty-eight.

Tender, to be allowed in payment. Sect. 62. Any sum which has been tendered and is in the hands or under the control of the person

---

* As amended by chapter 216, Public Laws of 1893.

owning or having charge of such land, shall be allowed in payment of said appraisal.

*Sect. 63. If the persons owning or having charge of the land on which such location is made, are dissatisfied with such appraisal, either party may within ten days appeal to the county commissioners of the county in which the land lies, by filing a copy of the proceedings and a claim of appeal with said commissioners, and the determination of a majority of said commissioners shall be final. *Land owners may appeal.*

*Sect. 64. When any town has erected or moved a building upon such lot or in any way improved the same, such improvement shall inure to the benefit of such town, and the same may be as completely occupied and controlled by such town as it would have been if such location had been in strict conformity to law. *Improvements, inure to town or district.*

Sect. 65. The legality of a tax assessed to build, repair or remove a schoolhouse and to pay for a lot, shall not be affected by any mistake or error in the designation or location thereof. *Tax, not effected by error in location.*

*Sect. 66. A plan for the erection or reconstruction of a schoolhouse voted by a town shall first be approved by the superintending school committee. *Plan, to be approved by S. S. committee.*

Sections 67 to 84 inclusive. (Repealed, except as applicable to districts not abolished by section 1 of chapter 216, Public Laws of 1893, and to precincts formed under provisions of section 7 of said chapter for the maintenance of free high schools.)

_____

* As amended by chapter 216, Public Laws of 1893.

POWERS AND DUTIES OF SUPERINTENDING SCHOOL COMMITTEES AND SUPERINTENDENTS.

Officers, to be sworn. *Sect. 85. Members of superintending school committees shall be sworn.

Terms of office, how fixed. *Sect. 86. School committees at their first meeting shall designate by lot a member or members to hold office for one, two and three years respectively, in manner as follows; one for one year, one for two years and one for three years; and they shall certify such designation to the town clerk to be by him recorded. Said committee shall have power to fill vacancies occurring during the interim between annual meetings, and the term of office of any member **—vacancies, how filled.** of the committee so chosen shall expire at the next annual town meeting. No member of the superintending school committee of any town shall be employed as a teacher in any public school in said town.'

(See Sect. 129.) †Sect. 87. The management of the schools and the custody and care of all school property in every town, shall devolve upon a superintending school committee which shall perform the following duties.

Appoint time and place for examination of teachers. †I. They shall appoint suitable times and places for the examination of candidates proposing to teach in town, and shall give notice thereof by posting the same in two or more public places within the town at least three weeks before the time of said examination, or by the publication of said notice for a like time in one or more newspapers having the largest circulation in the county. They shall employ teachers **—school week and month.** for the several districts in the town. Five days constitute the school week, and four weeks a school month.

Instructors of youth, examination of. ‡II. On satisfactory evidence that a candidate possesses a good moral character, and a temper and disposition suitable to be an instructor of youth, they shall examine him in reading, spelling, English

* As amended by chapter 216, Public Laws of 1893, and further amended by chapter 327, Public Laws of 1897.
† As amended by chapter 216, Public Laws of 1893.
‡ As amended by chapter 32, Public Laws of 1891 and chapter 267 Public Laws of 1885.

grammar, geography, history, arithmetic, book-keeping, civics, and physiology with special reference to the effects of alcoholic drinks, stimulants and narcotics upon the human system; and the elements of the natural sciences, especially as applied to **agriculture,** and such other branches as they **desire to introduce** into public schools, and particularly into the school for which he is examined; also as to his capacity **for** the government thereof.

*III. They shall **give to each candidate found** competent, a certificate that he is qualified to govern **said** school and instruct in the branches above **named,** and such other branches as may be necessary **to be** taught therein; **or** they may render valid by indorsement, any graded certificate issued **to teachers** by normal school principals, or the state superintendent. No certificate **shall** be granted **any person** to teach in the public schools of this state **after the** fourth day **of July,** eighteen hundred and **eighty-five,** who **has not** passed a satisfactory examination in **physiology** and hygiene, with special reference to **the effects** of alcoholic drinks, stimulants and narcotics **upon** the human system. *Certificate to teachers.*

IV. Direct the general course of instruction, and **select** a uniform system of text-books, due notice of which shall **be** given; any text-book thus **introduced,** shall not be changed for five years unless by a vote of the town; any person violating this provision shall forfeit not exceeding five hundred dollars, to be recovered in an action of debt **by any school** officer or **person** aggrieved. **And when said** committee shall **have made** such **selection of school-books,** they shall contract, under section eight, **with the** publishers for the purchase and delivery thereof, and make such rules as they deem effectual for their preservation and return. *Direct course of instruction and text-books.* *—purchase and preservation of books.*

*V. They shall make provisions for instructing all pupils in all schools supported by public money, *Make provisions for instruction in,*

* As amended by chapter 267, **Public Laws of 1885.**

—effects of alcoholic drinks, etc.

or under state control, in physiology and hygiene, with special reference to the effects of alcoholic drinks, stimulants and narcotics upon the human system.

May dismiss teachers for sufficient cause.

*VI. After due notice and investigation, they shall dismiss any teacher, although having the requisite certificate, who proves unfit to teach, or whose services they deem unprofitable to the school; and give to said teacher a certificate of dismissal and of the reasons therefor, a copy of which they shall retain, which shall not deprive the teacher of compensation for previous services.

Expel scholars.

VII. Expel any obstinately disobedient and disorderly scholar, after a proper investigation of his behavior, if found necessary for the peace and usefulness of the school; and restore him on satisfactory evidence of his repentance and amendment.

Exclude scholars not vaccinated.

VIII. Exclude, if they deem it expedient, any person not vaccinated, although otherwise entitled to admission.

IX. (Repealed by chapter 216, Public Laws of 1893.)

X. (Repealed by Chapter 199, Public Laws of 1893.)

Clasify scholars.

*XI. Determine what description of scholars shall attend each school, classify them, and transfer them from school to school where more than one school is kept at the same time.

Shall annually elect superintendent.

†XII. They shall annually elect a superintendent of schools who shall not be a member of the committee, who shall be ex-officio secretary of the committee. Said superintendent shall perform the following duties:

Duties of superintendent not a member of committee.

(1.) He shall make in April, annually, a certified list of the names and ages of all persons in his town, from four to twenty-one years, corrected to the first day of said month, leaving out of said enumeration all persons coming from other places to attend any college or academy, or to labor in any factory, or at any manufacturing or other business.

---

*As amended by chapter 216, Public Laws of 1893.
† As amended by chapter 216, Public Laws of 1893 and chapter 332, Public Laws of 1897.

(2.) He shall examine the schools and inquire into the regulations and discipline thereof and the proficiency of the scholars, **for which purpose he** shall visit each school at least twice each term.

(3.) He shall make all reports and returns relating to the schools of the town which are now or may be required by law to be made by superintending school committees.

(4.) He shall perform such other duties as said committee shall direct.

*Sect. 88. The superintendent of schools shall **annually** make a statement containing the following particulars. Annual statement.

I. The amount **of money** raised **and expended** for the support of schools, designating **what part is** raised by taxes, and what part from other funds, **and** how such funds accrued. Particulars.

II. The number of children between **four and** twenty-one years of age, belonging to their **town on** the first **day of April preceding.**

III. The whole number and the average **number** of scholars attending the summer schools; **the whole** number and the average, attending the winter schools, also the total number of different scholars attending school **two weeks** or more of the preceding **year, as** shall **appear from** the teachers' registers **returnable** to said officer agreeably to section ninety-six. Return of scholars.

IV. The average length of the summer schools in weeks; the average length of the **winter** schools in **weeks**; and the average length of the **schools** for the year.

V. The number **of male, and of female** teachers employed in the **public schools during any part of** the year.

VI. The wages of male teachers a month, and the wages of female teachers a week, exclusive of board.

†VII. He shall give **in his** returns the number of persons **between** the **ages of** four and twenty-one Returns, to superintend- ent of public schools.

---

* As amended by chapter 216, **Public** Laws of 1893.
† As amended by chapter 289, **Public** Laws of 1897.

years, corrected to the first day of April preceding the time of making said returns and full and complete answers to the inquiries contained in the blank forms furnished him by law; certify that such statement is true and correct, according to his best knowledge and belief; and transmit it to the office of the state superintendent on or before the first day of each May. He shall also furnish such other information relating to the public schools as the said superintendent shall at any time require of him.

Sections 89 and 90. (Repealed by chapter 216, Public Laws of 1893.)

Section 91. (Repealed by chapter 268, Public Laws of 1889.)

School committees, to serve without pay, unless otherwise voted by the town.

—pay of superintendent.

*Sect. 92. Superintending school committees shall serve without pay, unless otherwise voted by the town, but the superintendent shall receive for his services such sum as the town shall annually vote therefor, which sum shall in no case be less than two dollars per day for every day of actual service.

Sections 93, 94 and 95. (Repealed by chapter 216, Public Laws of 1893.)

DUTIES AND QUALIFICATIONS OF INSTRUCTORS.

Teachers, to keep school register.

—not to be paid till register is completed.

Sect. 96. Every teacher of a public school shall keep a register thereof, containing the names of all the scholars who enter the school, their ages, the date of each scholar's entering and leaving, the number of days during which each attended, the length of the school, the teacher's wages, a list of text-books used, and all other facts required by the blank form furnished him; such register shall at all times be open to the inspection of the school committee, and be returned to them at the close of the school. No teacher shall be paid for his services, until such register, properly filled, completed and signed, is deposited with the school committee, or with a person designated by them to receive it.

* As amended by chapter 216, Public Laws of 1893, and further amended by chapter 327, Public Laws of 1897.

*Sect. 97. The presidents, professors, and tutors of colleges, the preceptors and teachers of academies, and all other instructors of youth, in public or private institutions, shall use their best endeavors to impress on the minds of the children and youth committed to their care and instruction, the principles of morality and justice, and a sacred regard for truth; love of country, humanity, and a universal benevolence, sobriety, industry, and frugality; chastity, moderation, and temperance; and all other virtues which ornament human society; and to lead those under their care, as their ages and capacities admit, into a particular understanding of the tendency of such virtues to preserve and perfect a republican constitution, secure the blessings of liberty, and promote their future happiness; and the tendency of the opposite vices, to slavery, degradation and ruin. And it also shall be the duty of all teachers in the public schools of this state to devote not less than ten minutes of each week of the school term, to teaching to the children under their charge, the principles of kindness to birds and animals. *[Instructors of colleges, etc., to inculcate morality, justice and patriotism. —kindness to birds and animals, shall be taught in public schools.]*

†Sect. 98. Whoever teaches a public school without first obtaining a certificate from the school committee of the town, forfeits not exceeding the sum contracted for his daily wages, for each day he so teaches, and is barred from receiving pay therefor; and no certificate shall be valid for more than one year without the approval of the superintending school committee annually endorsed thereon. *[Forfeiture, for teaching without certificate.]*

SCHOOLS IN PLANTATIONS.

‡Sect. 99. Plantations have the same powers and liabilities as towns, for electing committees, treasurers, collectors, and for raising, assessing and collecting school-money, to be apportioned and expended as in towns. The assessors of plantations *[Powers of plantations.]*

* As amended by chapter 221, Public Laws of 1891.
† As amended by chapter 228, Public Laws of 1889.
‡ As amended by chapter 216, Public Laws of 1893.

may take a census of the inhabitants thereof, at the expense of the plantation, and when so taken, the money raised therein for schools shall be upon the basis of such census and not upon the census of the state.

SCHOOLING OF CHILDREN IN UNORGANIZED TOWNSHIPS.

Schooling of children in unincorporated townships.

* Sect. 100. Whenever in any unorganized township in this state there shall be two or more children between the ages of four and twenty-one years, the state superintendent of schools shall cause an enumeration of said children to be made, and returned to him, and shall provide for the schooling of said chil-

Enumeration of children in.

dren, either by establishing a school in the township, or by sending the children to schools in adjoining towns or plantations, or both, as shall by him be deemed expedient. In case any of said children are,

State superintendent may establish schools in township or send children to schools in adjoining towns.

by the state superintendent, sent to schools in adjoining towns or plantations, said children so sent shall have the same rights in such school as children resident in said town or plantation. Provided, however, that in case the interest on the reserve fund in any unorganized township together with the amount arising from the per capita tax called for in this act, is not sufficient to provide schooling for the children of said township for at least twenty weeks in a year, the

—expense of schools how paid.

remainder of the expense shall be paid from the fund appropriated by section four of this act, provided further, that no money shall be expended under this section for the benefit of any township until the inhabitants of said township shall pay to the state treasurer a sum equal to twenty-five cents for each inhabitant thereof.

The state superintendent shall certify to the governor and council the number and residence of the children enumerated and schooled, as provided in section one of this chapter, together with the cost of schooling said children and the governor and council

*As amended by chapter 83, Public Laws of 1899.

shall direct the treasurer of state to pay to the state superintendent of schools so much of the interest on the reserve land fund of the township in which said children reside as, added to the amount received from the inhabitants of the township from the per capita tax, shall pay the expense of said school. The state superintendent of schools shall pay to the treasurer of any town or plantation in which he may school any of said children, the same amount per scholar as is apportioned per scholar by the state treasurer for that year.

The state superintendent of schools shall have power to appoint agents for the several townships in which schools shall be established under this act, whose duty it shall be under the direction of the state superintendent to enumerate the pupils, collect the per capita tax, employ the teacher and attend to all necessary details in connection with said schools; for which work he shall be paid a sum not exceedisg two dollars per day, when actually employed in this duty, and actual necessary traveling expenses. *State superintendent of schools shall have power to appoint agents. Compensation of agents.*

For the purpose of carrying out the provisions of this act, there is hereby appropriated the sum of fifteen hundred dollars annually. *Appropriation.*

STATE SUPERINTENDENT OF PUBLIC SCHOOLS.

*Sect. 102. The governor with the advice and consent of council, shall appoint a state superintendent of public schools, who shall be sworn and continue in office three years, or during the pleasure of the executive; vacancies shall be filled by a new appointment for a like term. *Appointment and term of office.*

Sect. 103. An office shall be provided for him at the seat of government, where he shall preserve all school reports of this state and of other states which he may receive, the returns of the school committees of the various towns, and such books, apparatus, maps, charts, works on education, plans for school buildings, models, and other articles of interest to *To have an office at the capital.*

* As amended by chapter 237, Public Laws of 1897.

school officers and teachers as may be procured without expense to the state.

Duties.

Sect. 104. His duties are as follows:

To exercise general supervision of schools.

I. To exercise a general supervision of all the public schools, and to advise and direct the town committees in the discharge of their duties, by circular, letters and personal conference, devoting all his time to the duties of his office.

Obtain and disseminate information relating to school systems, etc.

II. To obtain information as to the school systems of other states and countries, and the condition and progress of common school education throughout the world; to disseminate this information, with such practical hints upon the conduct of schools and the true theory of education as observation and investigation convince him to be important, by public addresses, circulars, and articles prepared for the press; and to do all in his power to awaken and sustain an interest in education among the people, and to stimulate teachers to well directed efforts in their work.

Take necessary measures for holding state educational conventions.

III. To take such measures as he deems necessary to secure the holding of a state educational convention once each year, with a view of bringing together the teachers, school committees and friends of education, for consultation with reference to the interest of common schools and the most approved methods of instruction.

May hold county institutes.

IV. If sufficient encouragement is afforded by the citizens, to hold in each county once during each year a public meeting or institute for teachers and educators.

To publish abstracts of proceedings of such conventions.

V. To prepare and cause to be printed and distributed such portions of the proceedings of state institutes or teachers' conventions as he deems important in the furtherance of education.

Prescribe studies to be taught.

VI. To prescribe the studies to be taught in the common schools, reserving to town committees the right to prescribe additional studies.

State examination of teachers.

VII. To cause to be held, at such convenient times and places as he may from time to time designate, public examinations of candidates for the position of teacher in the public schools of the state. Such examinations shall test the professional as well as the scholastic abilities of the candidates, and shall be conducted by such persons and in such manner as he may from time to time designate. **Due notice of the** time, place and other conditions of the examinations shall be given in such public manner as he may determine.

To give a certificate of qualifications to all **candi-** dates who pass satisfactory examinations in such branches as are required by law to be taught, and who in other respects fulfill the proper requirements. Such certificate shall **be** either probationary **or permanent,** and shall indicate the grade of schools which the person named is qualified to teach. *[Certificates, issued to successful candidates.]*

To keep a list of approved candidates in **the office** of the state superintendent, and copies of **the same** with such information **as may** be desired **shall be** sent to school committees, **and** superintendents upon their **request.** *[List of candidates, at state superintendent's office.]*

The certificates issued under the provisions of this act shall be accepted by school committees, **and** superintendents in lieu of the personal examination **required by** section eighty-seven, chapter eleven **of the** revised statutes and all amendments thereto. *[Certificate, accepted in lieu of examination by S. S. committee.]*

*VIII. Annually, to report to the governor and council the **result of** his inquiries and investigations, and the facts **obtained** from the school **returns,** with such suggestions and recommendations **as in** his judgment would **best** promote the improvement of common schools. *[Make report to governor and council annually.]*

†IX. Biennially, **as soon as practicable after the** adjournment of **the legislature, to compile** and have **printed in** pamphlet **form, three thousand** copies of the amended school law of the state **and** distribute the **same to** the municipal and school officers of the several towns. *[To compile, publish and distribute amended school laws.]*

†X. To prepare and **issue** annually such circulars of information and advice to school officers, re- *[Issue circulars of information and]*

---

* As amended, 1893.
† As amended by chapter 307, Public Laws of 1889.

advice in
relation to
new laws.

lating to new school enactments, as he deems necessary for the intelligent and effectual enforcement of such enactments.

Furnish
blank record
books to
school
officers.

‡XI. The state superintendent shall furnish to the school officers of each town, proper blank books in which shall be kept complete and itemized records of all matters relating to moneys appropriated, received and expended for schools, which said books shall remain the property of the state.

Superintendent, to prepare and forward to town clerk blanks for school returns.

Sect. 105. Such superintendent shall prepare and print blank forms for all returns required by law, or deemed by him necessary, and shall, on the first day of each March, forward to town clerks, blanks for the annual school return, and registers for the school year commencing on the first day of April following; and said clerks shall forthwith deliver the same to the school committees of their towns.

To notify
delinquent
superintendents; also, to
return to
state
treasurer
number of
children
between 4
and 21.

*Sect. 106. He shall, on the first day of each June, notify the school superintendent of any town whose returns were not received at his office in May, and shall, annually, ascertain on the first day of July, the number of children between four and twenty-one years of age, in the towns from which returns are received, and furnish a list thereof to the treasurer of state.

†UNION OF TOWNS FOR EMPLOYMENT OF SUPERINTENDENT OF SCHOOLS.

Towns may
unite and
employ
superintendent.

I. On and after July first, eighteen hundred and ninety-seven, the school committees of two or more towns, having under their care and custody an aggregate of not less than twenty-five or more than fifty schools, may unite in the employment of a superintendent of schools, provided they have been so authorized by a vote of their towns at the regular town meetings, or special town meetings called for that purpose.

—committee
of towns

II. The school committee of the towns comprising a union shall form a joint committee, and for the

‡ Chapter 273, Public Laws of 1897.
* As amended by chapter 216, Public Laws of 1893.
† Chapter 296, Public Laws of 1897.

purposes of this act said joint committee shall be held to be the agents of each town comprising the union. Said joint committee shall meet annually at a day and place agreed upon by the chairman of the committees of the several towns comprising the union, and shall organize by the choice of a chairman and a secretary. They shall determine the relative amount of service to be performed by the superintendent in each town, fix his salary, apportion the amounts thereof to be paid by the several towns, which amounts shall be certified to the treasurers of said towns respectively; provided that the amounts so certified shall be in proportion to the amount of service performed in the several towns. They shall choose by ballot a superintendent of schools, in which choice the committee of each town shall have a vote proportional to the town's share of the expenditure for the superintendent's salary. *[uniting form a joint committee. —shall meet annually. —fix superintendent's salary and apportion amounts to be paid by each town. —choose by ballot a superintendent of schools]*

III. **Whenever the chairman** and secretary of said joint committee shall certify under oath to the state superintendent of public schools, (the form of certificate to be determined by said state superintendent,) in accordance with the provisions of this act, that a union has been effected as herein provided, that the towns unitedly have raised by taxation a sum not less than five hundred dollars for the support of a superintendent of schools, and that under the provision of this act a superintendent of schools has been employed for one year, then, upon the approval of said certificate by the state superintendent of public schools, and the presentation thereof to the governor and council, a warrant shall be drawn upon the treasurer of the state for the payment to the treasurers of the several towns of a sum equal to one-half the amount expended for superintendence by each of the several towns comprising the union, provided that not more than two hundred and fifty dollars shall be paid to any one town or more than seven hundred and fifty dollars to all the towns comprising any union. *[Amount to be raised by towns. —amount of state aid.]*

3

Salary, how
determined.

IV. The towns uniting for the purpose of employing a superintendent of schools shall appropriate for his salary their proportion of the sum paid said superintendent; and the amount to be paid by each town shall be determined by dividing the entire sum expended for superintendence among the towns comprising the union in the proportion of the service performed in each town.

Superintendents shall hold state certificates.

V. Persons employed to serve as superintendents of schools under this act shall hold state certificates under the act of eighteen hundred and ninety-five, providing for the state examination of teachers, and shall devote their entire time to superintendence.

Powers and duties of superintendents.

VI. The powers and duties of superintendents elected under this act shall be the same as those prescribed for town superintendents in chapter eleven, section eighty-seven of the public laws of the state of Maine.

Amount raised must be exclusive of common school fund.

VII. No town shall receive state aid under this act unless its appropriation and expenditure for superintendence have been exclusive of the amount required by law for common school purposes. If any part of the money raised by the towns or union of towns, or paid to them by the state for superintendence, is expended for any other purposes than those provided for in this act, then each person so misappropriating said money shall forfeit double the

Penalty for misappropriation.

sum so misapplied, to be recovered in an action of debt, in the name and to the use of the town, by any inhabitant thereof; and no town or union of towns shall receive further aid under this act until the amount so misapplied has been raised and expended for superintendence by such town or union of towns.

†TEACHERS' CONVENTIONS.

Teachers, may organize to hold conventions.

I. Whenever not less than thirty of the teachers and school officers of any county shall have formed an association under rules of government approved by the state superintendent of public schools, for

---

†Chapter 273, Public Laws of 1885, as amended by chapter 283, Public Laws of 1893.

the purpose of mutual improvement in the science
and art of teaching, and of creating popular interest
in, and diffusing a knowledge of the best methods of
improving our public school system, by the holding
of conventions at least once every year under the supervision of the state superintendent, the state shall
defray the necessary expenses attending the holding —state, to defray expenses.
of such conventions, for which purpose the sum of
one thousand dollars is hereby annually appropriated, to be deducted and set aside therefor by the
treasurer of state from the annual school-fund of the
state; *provided, however*, that no more than two such —proviso.
associations shall be formed in any county, and that
the expenses as aforesaid of no more than two conventions of any such association in any year shall be
defrayed by the state.

II.   Teachers of public schools are hereby author- Teachers, authorized
ized to suspend their schools for not more than two to suspend schools, and
days in any year during the sessions of such con- attend.
ventions within their counties, unless otherwise directed in writing by the school officers, and attend
said conventions without forfeiture of pay for the —proviso.
time of such attendance, provided they shall present
to the officers employing them, certificates signed by
the secretaries of such conventions and counter-
signed by the state superintendent of public
schools, showing such attendance.

III.   The governor and council are hereby au- Governor and council
thorized to draw warrants on the treasurer of state to draw warrants.
for the payment of bills for the expenses herein
provided for, when such bills shall have been approved by the state superintendent of public
schools; *provided, however*, that no bills shall be so —proviso.
paid except those for advertising such conventions,
and for actual traveling expenses of speakers and
lecturers not residing in the counties in which such
conventions are held.

NORMAL SCHOOLS.

Three normal schools, where located. Sect. 107. The northern normal school at Farmington, the eastern normal school at Castine, and the western normal school at Gorham, shall be conducted for the purposes and upon the principles herein set forth.

Their objects. I. They shall be thoroughly devoted to the training of teachers for their professional labors.

II. The course of study shall include the common English branches in thorough reviews, and such of the higher branches as are especially adapted to prepare teachers to conduct the mental, moral and physical education of their pupils.

III. The art of school management, including the best methods of government and instruction, shall have a prominent place in the daily exercise of said schools.

Christianity and morality to be taught. IV. Said schools, while teaching the fundamental truths of Christianity, and the great principles of morality, recognized by law, shall be free from all denominational teachings, and open to persons of different religious connections on terms of equality.

Principals of normal schools or normal departments in other schools, required to forward to superintendent statistics of students therein; and the information to be laid before the legislature. V. The principals of the normal schools and of all other schools in which normal departments are supported, wholly or in part, by the state, shall keep a register containing the names of all students entering such schools or departments, the date of entering and leaving, their ages, number of days attendance, the length of the term, a list of text-books used, and all other information required in the blanks furnished by the state superintendent. Such register and blanks shall be returned to said superintendent by the first day of each December, and the information so furnished shall appear in his annual report, for the use of the legislature.

Course of study, arranged by superintendent. Sect. 108. The course of study shall occupy two years with suitable vacations; and with the terms of admission shall be arranged by said superintendent, subject to the approval of the governor and council.

The trustees may arrange for a course of study, occupying **three or four years, for such** students as may elect to pursue the same. —trustees, may extend it.

Sect. 109. Any **student who completes the** course of study prescribed, and otherwise complies with the regulations of the school, **shall receive a** diploma certifying the same. Diplomas, provided for.

Sect. 110. Applicants for **admission shall be six**teen years of age if females, and seventeen **if males** and shall signify their intention to become teachers and come under obligation to teach in **this** state for at least one year, and if they receive a diploma, two years after they have graduated; on these conditions shall be received without charge for tuition; but each pupil shall pay one dollar and fifty cents for incidental expenses of the school. Applicants for admission, qualifications of. —tuition.

Sect. 111. Said schools **are under the direction of** a board of seven trustees, **five of whom shall be ap**pointed by the governor, with the advice and consent of the council, **for not more than three years under** one appointment; and the governor and superintendent of public schools **are, by virtue** of their office, members of the board. **Each of the** trustees appointed by the governor shall receive **ten cents** a mile for actual travel each way, and two dollars a day for his services when employed. **Said board** has charge of the general interests of said schools; shall see that **the affairs thereof are conducted as re**quired by law **and by** such by-laws as **the board** adopts; employ teachers and lecturers for the same; and annually on the first day of December **lay before** the governor and **council for the** information of the legislature, a financial statement, furnishing an accurate detailed account of the receipts and expenditures for the school year preceding. Trustees of normal schools, appointment of, etc. —term. —compensation. —powers and duties of. —report of.

*Sect. 112. For **support** of the three normal schools, **and the** Madawaska Training School, thirty-one thousand dollars is annually appropriated, to be expended under the direction of said trustees, Annual appropriation of $31,000.

* As amended by chapter 37, Public Laws of 1891.

—treasurer, to deduct same from school moneys.

which sum the treasurer of state shall deduct for said purpose from any school-money raised for the support of common schools. The governor and council may, from time to time, as they think proper, draw warrants therefor on said treasurer in favor of said trustees.

—governor, etc., may draw warrants in favor of trustees.

PENAL PROVISIONS AFFECTING SCHOOLS.

Forfeitures, how recovered and appropriated.

Sect. 113. Forfeitures under this chapter, not otherwise provided for, may be recovered by indictment, and shall be paid into the treasury of the town where they occurred, for the support of schools therein, in addition to the amount required by law to be raised; but the costs of prosecution shall be paid into the county treasury; any town neglecting for one year, so to expend such money, forfeits an equal sum to any person suing therefor in an action of debt.

—penalty of town for neglect to expend money.

Penalty for disturbing schools.

Sect. 114. Whoever, whether a scholar or not, enters any schoolhouse or other place of instruction, during or out of school hours, while the teacher or any pupil is present, and wilfully interrupts or disturbs the teacher or pupils by loud speaking, rude or indecent behavior, signs or gestures; or wilfully interrupts a school by prowling about the building, making noises, throwing missiles at the schoolhouse, or in any way disturbing the school, forfeits not less than two nor more than twenty dollars, to be recovered as aforesaid, or on complaint.

Parents or guardians, liable.

*Sect. 115. If a minor injures or aids in injuring any schoolhouse, outbuildings, utensils or appurtenances belonging thereto; defaces the walls, benches, seats, or other parts of said buildings by marks, cuts or otherwise; or injures or destroys any school property belonging to a town, such town by the truant officer thereof, or any one of them, may recover of his parent or guardian, in an action of debt, double the damage occasioned thereby.

---

* As amended by chapter 206, Public Laws of 1893.

Sect. 116. Whoever defaces the walls, benches, seats, blackboards, or other parts of any schoolhouse or outbuildings belonging thereto by obscene pictures, language, marks or descriptions, shall be fined not exceeding ten dollars, on complaint made within one year.

Penalty, for defacing school houses, outbuildings, etc.

STATE SCHOOL-FUNDS.

Sect. 117. The treasurer of state shall keep a separate account of all moneys received from sales of lands appropriated for the support of schools or from notes taken therefor, and of any other moneys appropriated for the same purpose; and such sum shall constitute a permanent school-fund, which may be put at interest as the legislature directs. A sum equal to six per cent of the amount of such fund, and all money received by the state from the tax on banks, together with one-half the amount of the annual tax paid by savings banks shall be annually appropriated to the support of common schools, and distributed among the several towns according to the number of children therein between four and twenty-one years of age.

Permanent school-fund.

Sect. 118. The treasurer shall, immediately after the first day of July, apportion to the towns all state school-funds for the year, according to the list of children furnished by the superintendent of public schools, as provided in section one hundred and six. The number of such children belonging to a town from which either the school committee or the municipal authorities have failed to make the returns required by law, shall be reckoned by taking the number used as a basis of the last apportionment, and deducting all such children set off to other towns, or incorporated into a new town within a year, and one-tenth of the remainder, and the residue shall be the basis of the new apportionment. Immediately after making the apportionments, the treasurer shall notify each town of its proportion; which shall not be paid to any town until its return is made to the superintendent of pub-

Treasurer, to apportion school-funds.

—basis, when returns are not received.

—not to be paid until return is made.

lic schools, nor so long as any state tax assessed upon such town remains unpaid.

Mill tax for support of schools. Sect. 119. A tax of one mill on a dollar shall annually be assessed upon all the property in the state according to the valuation thereof, and shall be known as the mill tax for the support of common schools.

How assessed and collected. Sect. 120. This tax shall be assessed and collected in the same manner as other state taxes, and be paid into the state treasury and designated as the school mill fund.

To be distributed in January annually. Sect. 121. This fund shall be distributed by the treasurer of state on the first day of January, annually, to the several cities, towns and plantations according to number of children therein, as the same shall appear from the official return made to the state superintendent for the preceding year.

Any portion unexpended, to be added to permanent school-fund. Sect. 122. All of the school mill fund not distributed or expended during the financial year shall at its close be added to the permanent school-fund.

PROVISIONS RESPECTING LITERARY INSTITUTIONS.

Presidents of colleges, tenure of office. Sect. 123. Presidents of colleges are removable at the pleasure of the trustees and overseers, whose concurrence is necessary for their election.

Fees for degrees conferred. Sect. 124. No officer of a college shall receive as perquisites any fees for a diploma or medical degree conferred by such college, but such fees shall be paid into the college treasury.

Innholders, stable keepers and certain others, not to give credit to students. Sect. 125. If an innholder, confectioner, or keeper of a shop, boarding-house or livery stable, gives credit for food, drink, or horse or carriage hire to any pupil of a college or literary institution in violation of its rules, or without the consent of its president or other officer authorized thereto by its government, he forfeits a sum equal to the amount so credited, whether it has been paid or not, to be recovered in an action of debt by the treasurer of such institution; half to its use, and half to the town where it is located; and no person shall be licensed by the municipal officers for any of said employments, if it appears that within the preceding year he had given credit contrary to the provisions hereof.

SCHOOL FOR THE BLIND.

* Sect. 126. Upon the request of the parents or guardians, the governor may, with the approval of the council, send such blind children as he may deem fit subjects for education, for a term not exceeding ten years, and thereafter in the discretion of the governor and council, in the case of any pupil, to the Perkins Institute for the Blind at South Boston, Massachusetts. In the exercise of the discretionary power conferred by this act, no distinction shall be made on account of the wealth or poverty of the parents or guardians of such children. No such pupil shall be withdrawn from such institution except with the consent of the proper authorities thereof or of the governor; and the sums necessary for the support and instruction of such pupils in such institution, including all traveling expenses of such pupils attending such institution shall be paid by the state; provided, however, that nothing herein contained shall be held to prevent the voluntary payment of the whole or any part of such sums by the parents or guardians of such pupils.

Governor and council, may send to Perkins Institute, South Boston, Mass.

LEGAL HOLIDAYS IN MAINE.

New Years Day, January 1; Washington's Birthday, February 22; Memorial Day, May 30; Independence Day, July 4; Labor's Holiday, 1st Monday in September; Christmas, December 25; Thanksgiving Day, Fast Day, appointed by the Governor and Council.

Legal holidays.

Arbor Day is a school holiday when observed for the purpose for which it is designated by the Governor and Council.

---

* As amended by chapter 2, Public Laws of 1899.

Sections 127 and 128. (Repealed by chapter 203, Public Laws of 1893.)

Superin-
tendent shall
not be a
member of
committee
*Sect. 129. The management of the schools and the custody and care including repairs and insurance on school-buildings, and of all school property in every town, shall devolve upon a superintending school committee which shall annually elect a su-
—towns may
elect super-
intendent.
perintendent of schools who shall not be a member of the committee, who shall be ex-officio secretary of the committee; but any town may elect a superintendent of schools by ballot at the regular town meeting.

*ALL EDUCATIONAL INSTITUTIONS RECEIVING STATE AID SHALL REPORT TO STATE SUPERINTENDENT.

Every educa-
tional institu-
tion receiving
State aid shall
report to
State super-
intendent.
I. Every educational institution receiving state aid, shall report to the state superintendent of public schools, the total and average attendance, receipts and expenditures, number of instructors, number and length of terms, with attendance for each, and answer such other questions as he shall determine, and the same shall be published in his annual report.

II. Every such educational institution failing to comply with the above requirements shall forfeit whatever aid or assistance it would otherwise receive from the state.

---

*Chapter 246, Public Laws of 1897.

INDEX TO LAWS.

COMPULSORY EDUCATION.

FREE HIGH SCHOOLS.

APPENDIX.

SUGGESTIONS, EXPLANATIONS AND FORMS.

SUGGESTIONS AND EXPLANATIONS.

SECT. 1.   The provision, that "the corporate powers of every school district shall continue under this act so far as the same may be necessary for the meeting of its liabilities and the enforcing of its rights," applies especially to those cases where districts have, under provisions of section 81, chapter 11, Revised Statutes of 1883, borrowed money to erect schoolhouses, etc., payable in annual instalments.   It continues in force, so far as those cases are concerned, the provisions of section 83, here quoted :

"Section 83.   At each annual assessment of town taxes after such loan, the assessors of the town shall assess the amount of the instalment and interest for that year, on the polls and estates in the district, as if the district had voted to raise it, and it shall, in like manner, be collected and paid to the town treasurer, who shall pay each instalment and interest as it becomes due on demand of the owner of the security."

SECT. 5.   The requirement, that "every town shall make provision for the maintenance of all its schools for not less than twenty weeks annually," does not modify or amend the provisions of section 6.   The two sections taken together require every town to raise for common schools, annually, not less than the sum provided for in section 6, and enough more to maintain all its schools as required in section 5, if more be necessary.

SECT. 9 and 10.   It is to be hoped and expected that under the new system, the carelessness in the distribution and care of text-books, which has prevailed in some towns, will cease. Now that the town owns and controls the schoolhouses, proper and safe receptacles should be put into every house in which to keep the books when not in use. Teachers should be held to strict accountability for keeping proper registers or records of their distribution to and return by pupils. Parents should be strictly required to make good all unnecessary injury to or loss of books by their children. All books, except in very exceptional cases and then only by express permission of superintendent, should be given up by pupils at the end of every term. Books seriously defaced, or injured beyond ready repair, should be discarded from use, and new ones supplied. If proper rules be made by school boards for the management of these matters, and those rules be strictly enforced, the almost criminal unsystem which has prevailed in certain towns, can be very easily corrected.

Sect. 17. Under the new system, the school board or some member thereof authorized to do so, must avouch for or approve all bills, before the municipal officers can legally draw orders for their payment. In most cases the superintendent should be so authorized, or the superintendent in connection with one member of the subcommittee of the board under whose authority any particular bill has been contracted.

Sect. 21. The provision of chapter 162, Public Laws of 1893, herein incorporated, that, "the age of pupils allowed to attend the public schools of this state is hereby fixed between the ages of five and twenty-one years of age," was not intended to change and does not change the basis upon which state school-moneys are apportioned to towns. That basis continues to be as prescribed in section 106, "the number of children between four and twenty-one years of age," as they existed in each town on the first day of April preceding. The provision was intended only to fix definitely by statute, what no previous statute had fixed, the age at and during which all children should have an enforceable right to attend the public schools.

Sect. 33. When a free high school precinct, formed in accordance with section 7 of chapter 216, Public Laws of 1893, votes to raise money by taxation for either of the purposes named in this section, as it may by the terms of said section 7, such money may be assessed and collected in the manner prescribed in sections 75 to 79 inclusive, chapter 11, Revised Statutes of 1883, which are here quoted:

"Section 75. When a district votes to raise money for any legal purpose, its clerk shall **forthwith, or within the time** prescribed by the district, certify the amount thereof to the **assessors** of the town, and the time when it must be raised; and within sixty days after receiving such certificate they shall assess it **as** they do town taxes, on the polls and estates of the residents and owners in the district at the time of raising said money, whether wholly in their town or not, and on the non-resident real estate in the district. They shall then make their warrant in due form of law, directed to any collector of their town or of the district, if any, if not to a constable, requiring **him** to levy and collect such tax and pay it to the town treasurer within the time limited in the warrant; and they shall give a certificate of the assessment to such treasurer **and** may abate such taxes as in the case of town taxes.

"Section 76. The assessors may include in their assessment such sum over and above the sum committed to them to assess, not exceeding five per cent thereof, as a fractional division renders necessary, and certify that fact to the town treasurer.

"Section 77. The town treasurer shall pay the expense of assessing and collecting any school district tax out of the money of the district, upon the order of the selectmen.

"Section 78. Section one hundred and forty-two of chapter six, and all **other** sections relating to the same subject apply to taxes assessed **by** or for school districts, so far as applicable; but the district and not the town is liable.

"Section 79. The collector or constable, and the town treasurer, or treasurer and collector, if one person is both, each have the same powers and are subject to **the same** duties and obligations in relation to district taxes, as to town taxes; and they and the asessors shall be allowed by the district for their services, a compensation proportionate to what they receive from the town for similar services."

SECT. **87.** Items I, II and III. The duties of school committees **herein** prescribed, **may** be performed by the superintendent when so specially directed under the provision of chapter 216, section 8, Public Laws 1893, that he shall "perform such other duties as said committee shall direct." In such case it will be sufficient legal evidence of the teacher's examination, qualifications, and employment, if the certificate granted be signed by the superintendent alone, "per order of the committee." A definite record of the vote directing him to perform these duties, and all others which they "shall direct" him to perform, should be made.

SECT. 87. Item IV. A requirement by the superintending school committee, that the Protestant version of the Bible shall be read in public schools of their town, by scholars who are able to read, is not in violation of any constitutional provision, and is binding upon the members of the school, although composed of divers religious sects. Donahoe *vs.* Richards, 38 Me. 379.

SECT. 87. Item VI. The superintending school committee have no power to dismiss a schoolmaster, unless for one of the causes mentioned in Stat. 1821, Chap. 117, Sec. 3, providing that the "committee shall have power to dismiss any schoolmaster or mistress who shall be found incapable or unfit to teach any school," and this must be in writing, under their hands, specially assigning the cause of dismissal. Searsmont *vs.* Farwell, 3 Me. 450. When there are three members of the superintending school committee, two of them have no power to dismiss a master, under the provisions of Stat. 1834, Chap. 129, Sec. 3, unless due notice has been given to the third that he might attend and act with them. Jackson *vs.* Hampden, 16 Me. 184.

When after one day's notice to the teacher, the superintending school committee visited the school and made a full examination into charges against the teacher, and the teacher and his witnesses were fully heard, and no objection was made by him for want of due notice, nor any request for delay or to be heard further, the teacher thereby waived any objection to the notice if insufficient, and is not entitled to his wages for teaching after being notified by the committee of his dismissal as the result of such investigation. Woodbury *vs.* Knox, 74 Me. 462.

SECT. 87. Item XII. The requirements of section 8, chapter 216, Public Laws of 1893, that committees shall annually elect a superintendent, and that all returns shall be made by said superintendent, **are** obligatory. Failure to elect such superintendent would work forfeiture of state school money so long as such failure continued; for the state treasurer is expressly forbidden to pay over such money "to any town until its return is made to the superintendent of common schools," (section 118); **and** the superintendent of public schools cannot, except by practical violation of his oath of office, certify to the state treasurer the receipt of any return not made, as the law requires, by a superintendent so elected.

SECT. 114. If one over twenty-one years of age, voluntarily attends a **town school, and is** received as a scholar by the instructor, he has the **same** rights and duties, **and is** under the **same** restrictions and liabilities, **as** if under that age. Stevens *vs.* Fassett, 27 Me. 266. When a scholar in school hours, intrudes himself into the instructors's **desk, and** refuses to leave it on the request of the instructor, such scholar may be lawfully removed by the instructor. And for that **purpose, he** may immediately **use such force,** and call to his assistance such aid from any other **person, as is** necessary to accomplish the object, without the direction or knowledge of the superintending school committee.—*Ib.* The statute, 1850, chapter 193, article 10, section 13, (containing the provisions of section 114,) for the protection of schools, **is** applicable to **private** schools regularly established and in operation for instruction in the art of writing State *vs.* Leighton, 35; Me. 195.

A schoolmaster is not liable **for** inflicting corporal punishment upon a **pupil, if it is** not clearly excessive, in the general judgment of reasonable men. Patterson *vs.* Nutter, 78 Me. 509.

A board of superintending school committee cannot elect a superintendent of schools while there are vacancies existing in the board, or until those vacancies are legally filled. Strout, J., in case of town of Cumberland.

If a vacancy exists in the board of superintending school committee at the time of the annual town meeting and the town fails to elect a person to fill this vacancy, it must be filled by the remaining members of the board and cannot be filled by a special town meeting.

FORMS.

I. FREE HIGH SCHOOL PRECINCTS.

The application made to the municipal officers of the town for the calling of a meeting to form a free high school precinct, may be as follows:

To the selectmen of the town of............... :

You are hereby requested by the undersigned, legal voters of the town of........., resident in the section of said town hereinafter described, to call a meeting of the voters resident within the following described limits, to wit: (*here definitely describe the limits of the proposed precinct*) ; to be held at (*here name the place of meeting*) on the ....day of........., 189.., at .. o'clock in the ...., then and there to act upon the following articles:

1. To choose a moderator to preside at said meeting.

2. To choose a secretary for said meeting.

3. To see if said voters will establish said described section as a free high school precinct.

4. To choose an agent and clerk for said precinct.

5. To provide and appropriate such sums as may be deemed necessary for the support of a free high school within said precinct for the ensuing year.

6. To determine where said school shall be located or kept.

7. To act upon any other business which may legally come before said meeting.

Dated at said.........., the.......day of........, 189...

The notice for a meeting on the foregoing application may be in the form following:

To........, one of the inhabitants of the following described section of the town of..........., viz: (*Here recite the limits given in the foregoing application.*)

Greeting.—Written application having been made to the undersigned, municipal officers of said town, by (*here insert names of those signing application*), legal voters of said section, to call a meeting of the legal voters thereof at the time and place and for the purposes hereinafter named, you, the said........, are hereby required in the name of the State of Maine, to notify and warn the inhabitants of said section of the town of........, qualified by law to vote in town affairs, to meet at the (*here designate the place of meeting*) in said section (*here insert the time and purposes of the meeting as set forth in the application therefor.*)

Dated at........, the......day of ...., 189..

——————— ———————, Selectmen of———————.

The form of return (or certificate of notice) on the foregoing warrant may be as follows:

Pursuant to the within warrant, to me directed, I have notified and warned the inhabitants of the within described section, in the town of........, qualified as therein expressed, to assemble at the time and place and for the purposes therein expressed, by posting up an attested copy of said warrant at..........in said section, and at............, being public and conspicuous places in said section, on the......day of........, being seven days before said meeting.

Date the......day of........, 18..

II.

Certificate of superintending school committee of dismissal of a teacher.

The undersigned, superintending school committee of the town of........., met at the schoolhouse in *school No. ..., in said town, on the......day of..........., 18.., due notice of which time and place of meeting and the purposes thereof having been given to each member thereof and to the teacher in said district, and after careful and deliberate investigation, we do hereby certify that we deem the services of.........., now employed as a teacher in said district, *unprofitable to the school

---

* If schools are designated otherwise than by number, use such designation.

therein, and we accordingly dismiss said teacher for the reasons following, viz :

(Here insert the reasons of dismissal.)

Dated at said......, the....day of........, A. D. 18..

—— —— ——,

—— —— ——,

—— —— ——,

Supt. School Com. of.

III.

Certificate of Expulsion of a Scholar.

The undersigned, superintending school committee of the town of........., met at the schoolhouse in *school No. ...., in said town on the......day of........., 18.., due notice of which time and place of meeting and the purposes thereof having been given to each member of said committee, and after proper investigation of the behavior of........, a scholar in the school therein kept, we have adjudged that the said........is an obstinately disobedient and disorderly scholar, and that we deem it necessary for the peace and usefulness of the school that he be removed therefrom, and we accordingly expel the said ....from said school.

Dated at said......, the....day of..........A. D. 18..

—— —— ——,

—— —— ——,

—— —— ——,

Supt. School Com. of....

---

* If schools are designated otherwise than by number, use such designation.

www.ingramcontent.com/pod-product-compliance
Lightning Source LLC
Chambersburg PA
CBHW021636270326
41931CB00008B/1049